Linda Kaye's Birthdaybakers, Partymakers®

BAKE-A-CAKE
PARTY BOOK™

Special thanks to my children, Marcy and Mitchell, for inspiring so many fun ideas,
Susan Martin and Lori O'Neill for their invaluable assistance,
Eireann Corrigan and Katie Schullman for their special way with words,
Rebecca Russell for her cake artistry,
and my husband Bill for enthusiastically believing in this project.

Art direction and design by: 3+Co. (www.threeandco.com)
Illustration: Peter Elwell
Photography: Michael Cogliantry

First published in the United States in 2005 by
Linda Kaye's Birthdaybakers, Partymakers®
195 East 76th Street, New York, NY 10021
www.partymakers.com

ISBN 0-9759161-0-6

Printed in China through Global PSD

Linda Kaye's Birthdaybakers, Partymakers®

BAKE-A-CAKE PARTY BOOK™

A STEP-BY-STEP GUIDE TO MAKE BAKING THE CAKE THE PARTY ITSELF!

CAKE RECIPE BY ROSE LEVY BERANBAUM,
AWARD-WINNING AUTHOR OF *THE CAKE BIBLE*

CONTENTS

CONTENTS

G GET
HER AND
E A
KE!

SEE BACK POCKET FOR FUN-TO-FOLLOW CAKE & RECIPE CARDS!

BIRTHDAYBAKERS

I think I'll call it... Birthdaybakers.

It started with a strawberry shortcake.

One of my earliest memories is the day my mother made this dessert with my sister and me. I loved seeing the heavy cream fluff into white, whipped peaks. We had so much fun spreading the icing on the freshly baked cake. When it came time to serve our creation, it tasted even better than it smelled in the oven; it was even more delicious because we helped make it.

Many years later, as a busy mother of two young children, Marcy and Mitchell, I was faced with a predicament. I looked at the calendar and Marcy's sixth birthday was just two weeks away. I had no entertainment, no party theme, and I hadn't even ordered a cake! When this realization hit me, I happened to be with a baker friend. Thinking out of the box, *and out of panic*, I asked her, *"Why not make a party out of baking the birthday cake?"* She offered to help me lead the kids in baking and decorating. This took care of the entertainment and the birthday cake!

The success of my daughter's party was the inspiration for me to start *Birthdaybakers, Partymakers®* in 1976. We would arrive at the home of the party child with all of the equipment and ingredients to lead the party guests in baking and decorating the birthday cake. These parties became a great success!

In more than 25 years, we have done over 5,000 Bake-a-Cake birthday parties. I have watched children of all ages stir ingredients and lick frosting off their fingers while the aroma of sugar and butter wafted from a warm oven. I loved hearing their giggles and gasps as they admired the decorations they were creating with pastry bags.

I have received many requests from parents for the secret behind the success of this party, so here it is!

The *Bake-a-Cake Party Book* includes the original cake recipe created especially for us by Rose Levy Beranbaum, author of *The Cake Bible*. It includes party ideas, cake templates, and more for celebrations throughout the year.

This book is all you'll need to create memories that will stick around long after the last cake crumbs have disappeared.

Linda Kaye

THE BAKE-A-CAKE PARTY IS AS EASY AS 1...2...3...4!

1. Everyone participates in making the batter.

2. While the cake is baking, partybakers mix up a rainbow of pastry bag frosting colors.

3. While the cake is "chilling out" in the freezer, the pastry bags are filled and then passed around the baking table so each of the guests has a turn to make all the different flower designs.

4. The cake is iced and ready to be decorated with the children's floral creations.

ALL THIS CAN BE DONE IN ABOUT ONE HOUR!

You're having a party,
so where do you start?

A cake with a rainbow
or one with a heart?

Once you decide
what you're going to make,

Follow this plan
for your Bake-a-Cake!

8

PLANNING THE PARTY

PARTY COUNTDOWN

6-WEEK TIME LINE

THE BAKE-A-CAKE PARTY IS A UNIQUE CELEBRATION. PLANNING IT WITH YOUR CHILD CAN BE AS MUCH FUN AS THE PARTY ITSELF!

6 WEEKS

- Choose party date and time
- Make guest list with contact phone numbers

4 WEEKS

- Send out party invitations
- Secure a pair of helping hands to assist during the party

2 WEEKS

- Check Party Essentials (pg. 12) for kitchen utensils and cake batter, icing, and frosting ingredients
- Purchase paper goods and party favors

1 WEEK

- Make Buttercream Icing (pg. 25) and Pastry Bag Frosting (pg. 28)
- Check film and camera battery
- Check oven temperature to see if cake-baking time needs to be adjusted (pg. 56)

DAY BEFORE

- Set up Baking Table (pg. 21)
  - Set up Decorating Tray with all nonrefrigerated items (pg. 31)
- Check pastry bag frosting for smooth consistency (Rebeat if needed)
- Divide pastry bag frosting into five containers and add a dab of color to each (Cover frosting containers and refrigerate)
- Set out cake knife and serving plate
- Place 2 potholders near the oven
- For birthdays, put candles and matches in convenient, out-of-reach place

DAY OF THE PARTY

- Take butter and eggs out of the refrigerator approx. three hours before guests arrive
- Check freezer to be sure space can easily be cleared for 15 minutes (approx.) cake cooling
- Center rack in the oven and pre-heat to 375° a few minutes before the guest arrive
- Remove pastry bag frosting containers from refrigerator and place on decorating tray upon guests arrival

PARTY ESSENTIALS

CAKE DECORATING TOOLS

Icing spatula

3 gel food colors (red, yellow, blue)

4 drop flower pastry tips

1 lattice pastry tip

5-6 disposable (12") pastry bags

Visit www.partymakers.com for the Bake-A-Cake Birthday Party Kit containing all your party decorating needs and more!

LET'S GET TOGETHER AND BAKE A CAKE!

PARTY PANTRY

Two 9" baking pans

2 wooden mixing spoons

Measuring spoons

Rubber spatula

Dry measures (1/2, 1 cup)

Flour sifter or strainer

2 potholders

5 teaspoons

3 large mixing bowls

One 2-cup liquid measure

5 small bowls or 1lb. plastic containers

Cake knife

Ten 9" Parchment rounds

Small rubber bands

2 small pieces wax paper

Hand wipes

Candy for guessing game

Dental floss

INGREDIENTS CHECKLIST

2 layer cake and pastry bag frosting:

Unsalted butter (4 sticks)

Large eggs (2)

Milk (1 pint)

Salt (1 tsp)

Granulated sugar (1 cup)

Pure vanilla extract (1tbs + 1 tsp)

Double acting baking powder (2 tsp)

Cake flour (2 cups)

Confectioners sugar (3 boxes)

Cake recipe on pg. 17

Pastry Bag Frosting recipe on pg. 28

BUTTERCREAM ICING CHECKLIST

Chocolate icing:

Unsalted butter (2 sticks)

Milk (1/3 cup)

Confectioners sugar (One 16 oz. box)

Pure vanilla extract (2 tsp)

Salt (pinch)

Unsweetened baking cocoa (3/4 cup)

Vanilla icing:

Unsalted butter (2 sticks)

Milk (1/2 cup)

Confectioners sugar (Two 16 oz. boxes)

Pure vanilla extract (2 tsp)

Recipes on pg. 25

A two-layer cake
splits the baking in two

So each little chef
gets a job to do—

This makes it simple
to involve everyone,

So divide the cake baking
and double the fun!

BAKING THE CAKE

MAKING THE CAKE FROM SCRATCH

RECIPE BY
ROSE LEVY BERANBAUM

LAYER CAKE RECIPE

BY ROSE LEVY BERANBAUM

Yield: One 9" cake layer.
Each group of partybakers will make 1 layer, creating a 2-layer cake.

Center rack in oven. Preheat oven to 375°.

For butter mixture, mix the following in a bowl:
1/2 stick room temperature unsalted butter
1/2 cup granulated sugar

Add:
1 egg
1/2 teaspoon pure vanilla extract
Mix thoroughly and set aside.

Combine dry ingredients in a separate bowl:
1 teaspoon baking powder
1/2 teaspoon salt
1 cup cake or bleached flour
Stir together and set aside.

Sift dry ingredients into butter mixture and stir.

Gradually add:
1/3 cup milk
Beat until batter is smooth.

Pour batter into a well-greased and floured 9" baking pan and distribute evenly.
Bake at 375° for approximately 20 minutes. Cake is ready when toothpick or
strand of raw spaghetti stuck in center of cake comes out clean. Remove cake
and immediately place baking pan in freezer to chill for approx. 15 minutes.

See the Recipe Card in the back pocket for fun-to-follow Bake-A-Cake Party instructions.

RECIPE FOR SUCCESS

PRE-PARTY PREP

A. **UP TO 1 WEEK BEFORE PARTY**
   Buttercream Icing, pg. 25 (15 min)
   Pastry Bag Frosting, pg. 28 (15 min)

B. **DAY BEFORE PARTY**
   Decorating tray set-up, pg. 31 (15 min)
   Baking table set-up, pg. 21 (20 min)

THE KEYS TO A SUCCESSFUL BAKE-A-CAKE PARTY ARE PRE-PARTY PREPARATION AND INVOLVING ALL THE CHILDREN IN THE BAKING PROCESS.

Preparation: TV cooking shows make every recipe seem easy because the chefs have just the right amount of each ingredient and all the equipment at their fingertips. Following this concept is essential to the Bake-a-Cake party.
Be sure your equipment and premeasured ingredients are ready to go before the guests arrive. If you don't have multiples of equipment, use bowls or cups to hold ingredients. (See pg. 21 for table layout.)

Involving all the partybakers: A total of 8 children works best. Gather the children around the table. Have an even number stand on each side. Each group will create one layer of the two-layer cake. This automatically creates enough activity for all of the partybakers. Remember: When there is one job to do, make it for two!

BAKING WITH KIDS

WHEN THERE'S ONE JOB TO DO, MAKE IT FOR TWO!

- To prepare the pan for baking, have one child hold the pan while the other butters the sides completely. Switch and let one child hold the pan while the other butters the bottom of the pan. Use wax paper to spread the butter and keep hands squeaky clean!

- Let partybakers take turns adding ingredients to the bowl.

- When mixing, one partybaker holds the bowl or frosting container while the other child mixes. Have the children switch after they have counted up to the birthday host's age. 1, 2, 3, 4, 5... switch! Switching keeps the kids energized, enthusiastic, and excited at the prospect of trying a new job.

CHECK OUT THE RECIPE CARD FOR MORE TIPS LIKE THESE.

- Have one child scoop up the baking powder with a teaspoon while another levels off the ingredients with the icing spatula or their finger.

- It takes two partybakers to hold the pastry bags open when it's time for adults to fill them with colored frosting.

PARTY TIPS

TABLE TALK

• The table can be set up in any room in your home...not just the kitchen!

• A rectangular 5'- 6' table covered with a plastic tablecloth works best for the party. Be sure the table is an appropriate height for children to stand at and work.

• Your Bake-A-Cake table can double as your party table! Just put your party tablecloth underneath the plastic baking tablecloth.

• Bring the Recipe & Cake Card to the table as a step-by-step visual guide to making and decorating the cake.

• The children stand around the table to mix, measure, and make flowers.

FOR ADULTS ONLY

• All oven activities are strictly for adults.

• Pass out a damp cloth for partybakers to wipe their hands before beginning, and have it available throughout the party.

• Always pass the bowl to the partybaker rather than asking the child to come to the bowl. It prevents crowding around the table and helps keep track of whose turn it is.

• Adults should carry out delicate tasks such as cracking the egg and pouring the vanilla when making the batter with younger children.

• After vanilla is added to the batter, be sure to give each partybaker the chance to sniff the yummy scent.

BETWEEN MAKING THE FLOWERS AND TRANSFERRING THEM ONTO THE COOLED CAKE, READ A STORY OR PLAY A SHORT GAME!

BAKING TABLE LAYOUT

REMEMBER THE DAMP CLOTH FOR STICKY FINGERS!

Stir up the frosting
until the colors shine brightly.

Fill the pastry bags
and tie them up tightly.

Squeeze out a blossom.
In fact, squeeze a dozen.

Grow a buttercream garden
while the cake's in the oven.

DECORATING THE CAKE

THE ICING ON THE CAKE

To create a blank canvas for your pastry bag flowers, ice the cooled cake with buttercream icing, remembering to ice between the layers. See pg.57 for the proper way to ice a cake.

ICE THE TOP AND SIDES OF THE CAKE.

ICING RECIPES

CHOCOLATE
BUTTERCREAM ICING

Bake-a-Cake Birthday Cake,
Father's Day Fun, Halloween Candycake

Yield: Enough for two 9" cake layers
Prep time: 15 minutes

2 sticks room temp. unsalted butter
2 teaspoons vanilla extract
1/3 cup milk
One 16 oz. box confectioners sugar
3/4 cup Dutch processed cocoa
Pinch of salt

In a bowl, beat butter until light and fluffy.
Beat in vanilla and milk while gradually
adding confectioners sugar and cocoa.
Cover and refrigerate.

VANILLA
BUTTERCREAM ICING

Valentine's Day Hearts, Rainy Day
Bake-a-Cake, Slumber Party Patchwork,
Frosted Fairytale, Mother's Day Nosegay,
4th of July Pinwheel

Yield: Enough for two 9" cake layers
Prep time: 15 minutes

2 sticks room temp. unsalted butter
1/2 cup milk
2 tablespoons vanilla extract
Two 16 oz. boxes confectioners sugar

In a bowl, beat butter until light and fluffy.
Beat in vanilla and milk while gradually
adding confectioners sugar.
Cover and refrigerate.

MAKE AHEAD: UP TO ONE WEEK BEFORE PARTY.
CHECK FROSTING FOR SMOOTH CONSISTENCY. REBEAT IF NEEDED.

PASTRY BAGS AND TIPS

tip 1

Tips 1-4 are DROP FLOWER TIPS.

tip 2

tip 3

tip 4

tip 5

Lattice Tip: used for borders, swags, etc. Best applied directly to cake.

26

MAKING THE FLOWERS AND DESIGNS:

Drop flower tips are easy to use and create beautiful flowers. The opening at the end of each tip determines its design. As you can see on the opposite page, each tip can create several different designs if you change the angle of your hand or the pressure with which you squeeze the bag.

INSERTING THE PASTRY TIP:

To make sure the decorating tip fits exactly into the disposable pastry bag, line up the tip with the point on the bag and then, using scissors, cut the bag at the base of the tip. Fold down the sides of the bag about half way. Insert the tip and you'll have a perfect fit!

FILLING THE PASTRY BAG:

Fold down the sides about half way to create the opening. Fill the bag 3/4 full with pastry bag frosting to prevent it from coming out the top.

Gather the bag together where the frosting ends and close it with a rubber band.

MAKING FLOWERS WITH A PASTRY BAG:

Hold the bag with one hand positioned directly above the rubber band and your other hand above the pastry tip. Give the bag a gentle squeeze to see a flower bloom on the parchment paper then lift the bag's tip. Pass the bags around so everyone has a turn making flowers with the different colors of frosting.

Partybakers will create their flowers on parchment rounds to make the flowers easy to transfer onto the cake.

TRANSFERRING THE FLOWERS ONTO THE CAKE:

A small icing spatula makes it easy to transfer your partybakers' favorite creations onto the cake. Use it to pick up each flower from their grouping of floral creations and another flat utensil to slide the flower onto the cake.

PASTRY BAG FROSTING

Yield: Enough to fill five 12" pastry bags

Prep time: 15 minutes

3 sticks room temp. unsalted butter

1 tablespoon pure vanilla extract

1/2 cup plus 1 tablespoon milk

Three 16 oz. boxes confectioners sugar

In a large mixing bowl, beat butter until light and fluffy. Beat in vanilla and milk while gradually adding confectioners sugar. Beat well. Cover and refrigerate.

MAKE AHEAD: UP TO ONE WEEK BEFORE PARTY

PASTRY BAG FROSTING PALETTE

Before the party, fill 5 containers about half way with pastry bag frosting and add a dab of food color to each. Partybakers will stir in the color on the day of the party. Add the following food colors to white pastry bag frosting to create these colors. Your child will choose 5 favorites for the party!

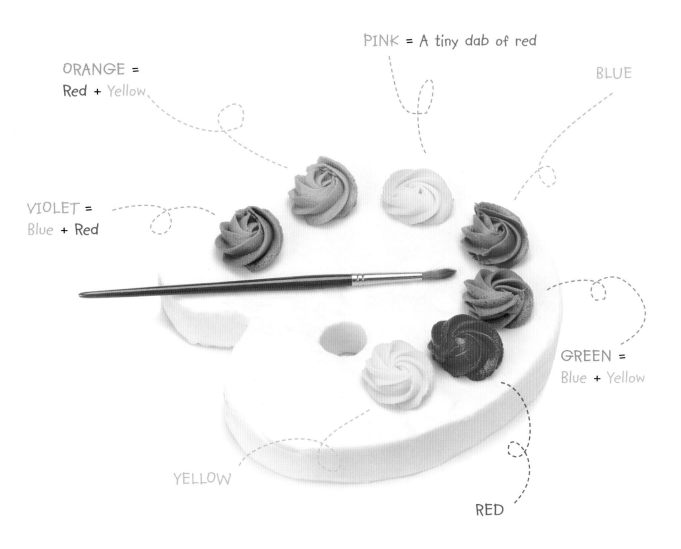

PINK = A tiny dab of red

ORANGE =
Red + Yellow

BLUE

VIOLET =
Blue + Red

GREEN =
Blue + Yellow

YELLOW

RED

CAKE DECORATING TRAY

Group these items together *before* the day of the party to ensure a smooth transition *between* baking the cake and making the flowers.

5 containers filled with pastry bag frosting

Five to six 12" pastry bags assembled with tips

Eight 9" parchment circles or wax paper squares

5 teaspoons for stirring frosting

1 small icing spatula, plus 1 flat utensil

4-6 small rubber bands

3 food color gels (red, yellow, blue)

HELPFUL HINTS

1. Pre-made pastry bag frosting may harden in refrigerator; simply re-beat to regain a smooth consistency before dividing into containers.

2. Add a dab of color to each container. Remember that a little goes a long way. Partybakers will stir in color during the party. See pg. 29 for Frosting Palette.

3. To write a message on the cake, fill a pastry bag with colored frosting and snip off the very end of the bag, then write message directly on cake.

DECORATING TRAY

1lb. CLEAR CONTAINERS

5 TEASPOONS

8 PARCHMENT CIRCLES

5 PASTRY BAGS WITH TIPS

3 FOOD COLOR GELS

4-6 RUBBER BANDS

1 ICING SPATULA

You will need 1 additional flat utensil to slide the flowers from the icing spatula onto the cake.

Guessing games, invitations,
decorations galore!

Flip through these pages
for fun cakes and more.

Pick which you want,
then take a look

At the easy directions
in the back of the book!

THEMED BAKE-A-CAKES & PARTY IDEAS

BIRTHDAY CAKES

MAKE-A-WISH CAKE

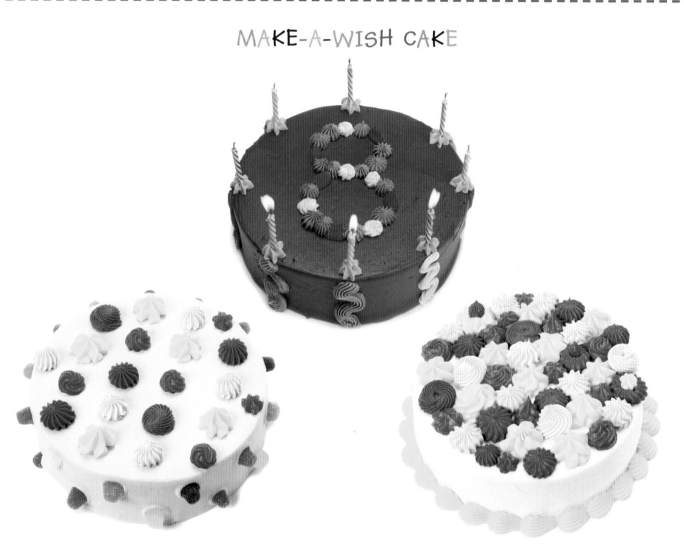

POLKA-DOT CANDYCAKE

BUTTERCREAM BOUQUET

HAPPY BIRTHDAY BAKE-A-CAKE

A GOOD OLD-FASHIONED BIRTHDAY PARTY!

PARTY SETTING: Use your child's favorite colors to make the party room a festival of fun! Hang bright streamers on the walls and tie vibrant balloons to each chair. Attach classic games, like Pin the Tail on the Donkey, to one of the walls for a trip down memory lane. Scatter jellybeans on the party table to add some sweet confetti. Then bring out the partybakers cake creation and set it in the middle of the table—a perfect birthday table centerpiece!

PARTY TREAT: Create a sundae bar and let the partybakers make their own ice-cream delights! Set up a confectionary table with lots of candy toppings and fluffy whipped cream for the sundaes.

CANDY GUESSING GAME: How many jellybeans can squeeze into a pastry bag?

PARTY FAVOR FUN: Add some excitement to the end of the party with a party favor grab bag! Let each child choose a number out of a hat to establish an order of picking and then let the fun begin! Children close their eyes and pick a favor out of the bag. Make sure you've chosen a variety of age-appropriate party favors that are sure to please, and leave time at the end of the party for a favor swap!

SPECIAL FUN: After all the guests have gone home, avoid the after party blues with a treasure hunt for gifts. Take a picture of your child opening each gift and send it along with the thank-you note.

FROSTED FAIRYTALE

CAKE TEMPLATE ON PG. 61

FAIRYTALE PARTY

. . . AND THEY BAKED HAPPILY EVER AFTER!

INVITATION: Announce your royal party with small parchment scrolls rolled up and tied with ribbons.

PARTY SETTING: Roll out the red carpet or create a yellow brick road for your guests to follow to your front door where the fairytale begins. Announce your guests' arrival with a trumpet blare and give tiaras and crowns to all the girls and boys in attendance. Once the guests have their regal headwear, invite them into the party room where the royal table awaits, lined with a fairytale table cover and sprinkled with shimmering flecks of glitter. The center of the table dazzles with a bouquet of giant lollipops, perfect for any prince or princess. After the party, the lollipops become magic wands for the guests to bring home to continue the magic long after the party is over.

CANDY GUESSING GAME: Use foil-wrapped candy kisses! Packed in a pastry bag, they will sparkle like jewels!

PARTY FUN: Invite your child's favorite fairytale character to help stir up some fun at the party! Use a hand puppet of the character to add some entertaining comments throughout the baking. Then, while the cake is baking, have the character read a favorite fairytale aloud to the party guests.

PARTY BEVERAGE: Plastic champagne flutes filled with sparkling apple cider add a final touch of elegance to this party fit for kings and queens or someone turning sweet sixteen.

FATHER'S DAY FUN

CAKE TEMPLATE ON PG. 63

FATHER'S DAY FAMILY FUN

HOW DO YOU SPELL FUN? D-A-D!

INVITATION: Make it a family event...no invitations necessary!

PARTY SETTING: There's no question about who is the star of the day...D-A-D designed in a very special way! Surprise the "Man of the Hour" with breakfast-in-bed made up of Dad's favorite foods, accompanied by his favorite newspaper. Remind Dad that he's king with his very own gold crown! Top it all off with a presentation of the delicious buttercream cake, baked with love, especially for him!

PARTY TIP: The family fun begins the day before. Gather family members to bake and decorate the cake for Dad. If there are less than four people, skip the baking table layout, double the cake batter recipe, and fill each baking pan 1/2 full with cake batter. Then proceed with the template directions. Otherwise, follow the recipe cards for a step-by-step guide to making this super special D-A-D cake. Make the cake even more special by choosing a giftwrap that reflects Dad's favorite hobbies and wrap the cardboard base for the sculptured cake letters with it.

PARTY FUN: It's time for a Father's Day Barbecue! Prepare Dad's favorite summer foods and eat outside if possible! Then, after dinner, play some of Dad's favorite board games or cards. For the grand finale, serve the special cake to the guest of honor!

PARTY EXTRAS: Present Dad with a scrapbook of pictures of special moments you shared together. (This will be a gift that DAD will long remember.)

4TH OF JULY PINWHEEL

CAKE TEMPLATE ON PG. 65

4TH OF JULY PARTY

INVITATION: Invite guests to arrive dressed in red, white, and blue.

PARTY SETTING: Greet guests at the door with the sounds of some good old American favorites – "America the Beautiful" and "Yankee Doodle Dandy"– it will get party guests in the mood to celebrate! For an extra splash of patriotism, plant pinwheels in patriotic colors in flowerpots around the party area. And finally, remember to proudly display Ole Glory in all her finest!

GUESSING GAME: Yankee Doodle may have preferred macaroni, but guessing the number of red, white, and blue jellybeans in a pastry bag tastes even more dandy!

PARTY FUN: Celebrate America the Beautiful with your very own parade. Pass out pots and pans to all the patriotic bakers with the party host leading the all-American procession.

PARTY TREATS AND EATS: A classic American barbecue is the perfect partner for this party. Keep it casual by writing the simple menu on a blackboard – hot dogs, burgers, and chips. Prop the board by the party table so guests can "order" their meal. For an extra sweet treat to go along with the Pinwheel Cake, arrange for an ice-cream truck to swing by the party and let the guests have their pick!

HALLOWEEN CANDYCAKE

CAKE TEMPLATE ON PG. 67

HALLOWEEN PARTY

INVITATION: Conjure up a guest list of little ghosts and goblins. Invite your child's friends to come dressed in their favorite Halloween costumes.

PARTY SETTING: Create a spooky spectacular from the moment the party begins! Play a sound track of creepy tunes to greet the guests as they arrive. The monster music will fill the air as they pass the white-sheet ghost that you've hung near your front door. A sign that reads "Enter at your own risk" beckons the party guests into the party room and heightens their eerie expectations. Baby pumpkins are set at each child's place, and a large jack-o-lantern pumpkin is the centerpiece. The napkins on the party table are tied with strings of black licorice for an extra treat, and candy corn and plastic spider rings are scattered across the party table. Light bulbs of gory green or hair-raising orange cast a ghoulish glow.

GUESSING GAME: Fill a pastry bag with candy corn and ask the guests to take a guess at how many sweet treats are in the bag.

PARTY FUN: (Create a story with each of the costumed guests starring as a character.) After story time, scare up a prize for every contestant at a creepy costume pageant. Lead a parade around the room for the costume judging. Categories like "Most Original," "Scariest," "Funniest," and "Most Popular Character," make each contestant a winner! Give out Halloween stickers and toys rather than candy… they'll get enough of that before the holiday is over! Take a picture with an instant camera of all the costumed guests to give them as a special take home favor.

PARTY BEVERAGE: Mix up a cauldron of bubbling witches brew made from orange soda and lime green sherbet.

ICE-CREAM CONE CUPCAKES

ICE-CREAM SOCIAL

I SCREAM, YOU SCREAM, IT'S ALL ABOUT ICE CREAM!

INVITATION: Invitations featuring a jukebox or an ice-cream soda will be a perfect start to this nostalgic Bake-a-Cake occasion.

PARTY SETTING: Create the feeling of this special Ice-Cream Social the moment your guests arrive, with music from the 50s playing in the background. Ask the boys to come wearing jeans with white t-shirts (rolled up sleeves are a must!) and have girls wear skirts and bobby socks. Set the party table with a red and white striped table cover (a white cover with stripes made of red streamers will do the trick.) Make old-fashioned soda Shop signs: "Ice Cream—5 cents!" or "Get a refreshing root beer float here!", and don't forget the one listing all the sweet flavors your guests can choose from!

GUESSING GAME: Ask your guests to twist on over to the blind ice-cream taste test. Guests should cover their eyes and guess which ice-cream flavor they are tasting after each delicious spoonful.

PARTY DRINKS: Root beer floats and cherry or vanilla cola are all perfect accompaniments to the party. Let the guests add the ice cream and watch it froth up into a delicious treat!

PARTY FUN: Break the kids into two teams and bring out the video camera! Each group makes a new formula for an ice-cream soda, using as many different ingredients as they want! After they name their creation, let the camera roll as each team films a commercial to sell their ice-cream soda concoction! Once everyone has had enough ice cream, it's time to watch the commercials as they enjoy the yummy ice-cream cone cupcakes.

MOTHER'S DAY NOSEGAY

MOTHER'S DAY TEA PARTY

TEA FOR TWO OR FOUR OR MORE...A BAKE-A-CAKE TEA PARTY WITH FUN GALORE!

INVITATION: An elegant invitation made out of a white doily will be the perfect beginning to this holiday tea party.

PARTY SETTING: Place a silver tea set in the center of the party table. Fill the teapot with roses, a beautiful flower for this springtime celebration. This will make a special addition to the party table. Later, the roses become party favors for all to enjoy! Moms and kids can each "pick" a flower to take home with them.

PARTY FUN: Team up party guests and their moms for a game show about themselves! Put a maternal twist on the classic "Newlywed Game" and quiz the moms about their children and the children about their moms. See which duo knows the most about each other. Ask questions like "What's your mom's favorite food?" or "Who's your child's favorite super-hero?"

GUESSING GAME: Have each mom bring a picture of herself as a baby. Then display the pictures and ask everyone to guess who's who!

PARTY BEVERAGE: Tea, of course! Have an array of herbal teas for the adults and the kids to enjoy along with their beautiful Mother's Day Nosegay cake!

PARTY TIP: Schedule the party around 3 p.m. or a day or two before Mother's Day to avoid conflicting with your guests' family obligations.

RAINY DAY CAKE

CAKE TEMPLATE ON PG. 69

RAINY DAY PARTY

NEED A REASON TO CELEBRATE WITH SOME IMPROMPTU BAKING FUN? HOW ABOUT A RAINY DAY BAKING EXTRAVAGANZA?

INVITATION: For this kind of last-minute festivity, a phone invitation is the way to go!

PARTY SETTING: Invite your guests to brighten up the rainy day by coming to the party dressed head-to-toe in their favorite sunshiney colors! Set a rainbow of crayons at each child's place and let them create their own sunny-day scene on the white paper table cover. It's fun to mix and match with paper goods you have on hand. A variety of plates, cups, and napkins will create a fun and vibrant table setting to lighten any gloomy day.

GUESSING GAME: An assortment of candies in every color of the rainbow is sure to brighten any rainy day. A "pot of gold" is the perfect rainy day container.

PARTY BEVERAGE: A colorful fruit punch or juice served in clear plastic cups will add even more cheer to your party table. Top off the fun with a paper umbrella in each child's cup! A cube of fresh fruit will keep the umbrella from "blowing away!"

PARTY TIP: Be prepared for stormy weather. Keep a large roll of butcher paper on hand for an instant table cover, and reserve a corner of a closet or pantry for storing leftover party supplies. This way, spontaneous gatherings can be a snap when the first raindrops begin to fall.

SLUMBER PARTY PATCHWORK

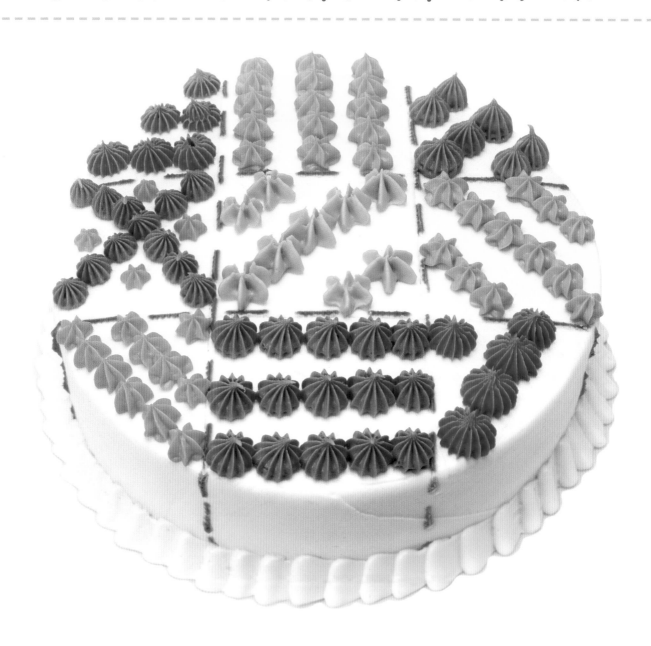

SLUMBER PARTY

INVITATION: Invite everyone to dress in pajamas and bring a favorite stuffed animal to spend the night!

PARTY SETTING: Place a pillowcase near the entrance to the party and ask everyone to autograph it with colored fabric markers...don't forget to add the date of the party! A teddy bear with a sleeping cap makes a cozy centerpiece for the party table. (Place a colorful sock over one ear for a cute cap!) Tie helium balloons to the teddy's paw to add a splash of color. Create a starry night by arranging glow-in-the-dark stars on the ceiling in the party hosts bedroom.

CANDY GUESSING GAME: Fill a pastry bag with marshmallows. These sugary pillows are perfect for a sleepover!

PARTY FUN: Lights! Camera! Action! It's time for the Bake-a-Cake Cooking Show! Take out your video camera and tape the cake-baking event. The party host acts as head chef as each guest plays their part adding, mixing, stirring, and measuring the ingredients for this patchwork quilt cake! Partybakers get to watch themselves in action! They can eat their delicious patchwork creation while the tape rolls! The grand finale is a late night awards show complete with trophies for categories such as "Best Flower Creation in a Cooking or Gardening Show."

PARTY TREATS: Set up a treat station with the party host's favorite candies. The guests can make their own treat bags to bring to the Bake-a-Cake Cooking Show premiere. With all of this sweetness, party guests are sure to have sweet dreams.

VALENTINE's DAY HEARTS

CAKE TEMPLATE ON PG. 71

VALENTINE'S DAY PARTY

INVITATION: Sweeten up the invitation by sending along a small heart-shaped box of chocolates.

PARTY SETTING: Invite the partygoers to help "decorate" the room by dressing in pinks and reds. A vase with pink roses will make an elegant centerpiece, and the pale pink buds will inspire the guests to create their own delicate buttercream blossoms. Scatter red rose petals on the party table for a dreamy accent to the décor, and switch your usual light bulbs to pink ones to cast a rosy glow in the room. For an extra touch of Valentine's Day charm, use large doilies as placemats and tie the napkins with bows made of red licorice strings.

CANDY GUESSING GAME: Fill a pastry bag with pink, red, and silver foil-wrapped candy kisses!

VALENTINE'S DAY MENU: Think pink and red when planning the menu! Use cookie-cutters to make heart shaped sandwiches filled with strawberry cream cheese. A silver bowl filled with fresh strawberries adds that special touch, especially when accompanied by a plate of confectioners sugar for dipping.

PARTY BEVERAGE: Mix up a pretty-in-pink punch with ginger ale and strawberry sherbet. Adults can sip on pink champagne as they toast the cake creation of their budding chefs.

PARTY FUN: Let the children select from a trunk filled with pearls, boas, and hats before they sit down to enjoy their special cake! This fanciful dress may even inspire a visit from Prince Charming himself!

What's the secret to this?
Why should I do that?

What could ruin the frosting?
Cause the cake to fall flat?

Why use cake flour?
What's a spatula do?

The following pages
hold the answers for you!

FREQUENTLY ASKED QUESTIONS

BAKING BASICS

HOW MANY PEOPLE CAN A 9" PARTY CAKE SERVE?

As many as 16, depending on the portions. To get the maximum number of servings, cut a circle in the cake center and slice pieces from its radius, then two more from the inner circle. Remember to cut the cake into age-appropriate slices!

WHAT'S THE DIFFERENCE BETWEEN CAKE FLOUR AND REGULAR FLOUR?

Cake flour will result in a fluffier cake. If cake flour is unavailable, you can use bleached flour.

HOW CAN I TELL WHEN THE BUTTER IS AT ROOM TEMPERATURE?

If pressing your thumb leaves an indentation, then the butter is just right!

WHY DO I NEED THE EGGS AND BUTTER TO BE AT ROOM TEMPERATURE?

Both will combine better with the other ingredients and will be easier to blend without the use of an electric mixer.

HOW CAN I BE SURE THAT MY BAKING POWDER IS FRESH?

Put 1/2 teaspoon into a cup of warm water. If it foams immediately, it is fresh and will do the trick! Your cake will be sure to rise.

HOW DO I CHECK MY OVEN TEMPERATURE?

Test it with a calibrator or oven thermometer, available at most supermarkets and hardware stores. To ensure 20 minute baking time, you may have to decrease the oven temperature if your oven runs hot, and if it runs cool, you may have to increase the oven temperature.

BAKING BASICS

HOW CAN I TEST IF THE CAKE IS READY TO COME OUT OF THE OVEN?

A toothpick or strand of raw spaghetti inserted into the cake should come out dry and the sides of the cake will begin to separate from the edges of the pan.

HOW DO I ENSURE SMOOTH ICING AND FROSTING CONSISTENCY AFTER REMOVING THEM FROM THE REFRIGERATOR?

Simply rebeat it to regain smooth consistency.

WHAT IS THE PROPER WAY TO ICE A CAKE?

Ice the top of one layer, then place the other layer on top, sandwiching the cakes together with icing. Using an icing spatula apply a liberal amount of icing to the top of the cake and spread it evenly over the top and sides, creating a smooth surface.

WHY DO I PUT THE CAKE IN THE FREEZER AFTER IT COMES OUT OF THE OVEN DURING THE BAKE-A-CAKE PARTY?

The cake must be cool for icing to adhere to it. Placing the cake pan in the freezer is the fastest way to cool it. The faster your cake is iced, the sooner the partybakers can add their floral creations to the cake top.

UTENSIL GLOSSARY

Icing spatula

Liquid measure

Measuring spoons

BAKE A CAKE BIRTHDAY PARTY KIT: Contains five 12" disposable pastry bags, 4 drop flower tips, 3 gel food colors, 2 paper baking pans, icing spatula, 8 Bake-A-Cake Party invitations, 8 chef diplomas, illustrated Recipe Card and Guide to make baking the cake the party itself! Available at www.partymakers.com.

DECORATING TIPS: Come in a variety of shapes and sizes. The opening at the end of each pastry tip determines its design. These tips are inserted into the snipped end of the disposable pastry bag. Drop flower tips are best for the party because they are easy to use and create beautiful flowers. A lattice tip creates great borders and swags.

12" DISPOSABLE PASTRY BAG: Clear, flexible, plastic, cone-shaped bag. Disposable bags make clean-up easier. Bag should be filled 3/4 of the way with pastry bag frosting.

DRY MEASURES: Measuring cups that come in sets of different sizes. Used to accurately measure dry, granular ingredients such as flour or sugar.

ICING SPATULA: A small metal spatula. Used for smoothing the top of the batter before the cake is baked and for icing the cakes. It is also to be used to transfer buttercream flowers onto the cake.

LIQUID MEASURE: A measuring cup with a spout for pouring. Place cup on a flat surface when filling.

UTENSIL GLOSSARY

MEASURING SPOONS: A graduated set of spoons. Best for measuring smaller amounts of ingredients, such as baking powder and vanilla.

MIXING BOWL: Sturdy bowl with a five-or-six cup capacity. Glass or metal is preferable as plastic can absorb odors.

PARCHMENT ROUNDS: Special paper that prevents cake from sticking to the pan. It is also the perfect surface for partybakers to practice making their flowers…it's even shaped like the top of the cake!

PLASTIC CONTAINERS: One-pound clear plastic containers used by delis and groceries. Disposable containers make clean up easier. You'll need five containers to store the pastry bag frosting for this party.

RUBBER SPATULA: Excellent for scraping batter out of mixing bowls.

SIFTER/STRAINER: Aerates the ingredients to make cakes lighter and moister by straining lumps that may have formed. A wooden spoon is needed if using a strainer to help sift dry ingredients into the bowl.

WOODEN SPOON: Spoon for mixing and blending ingredients.

These items are available at most hardware or kitchen stores.

Rubber spatula

Mixing bowl

Wooden spoons

FROSTED FAIRYTALE

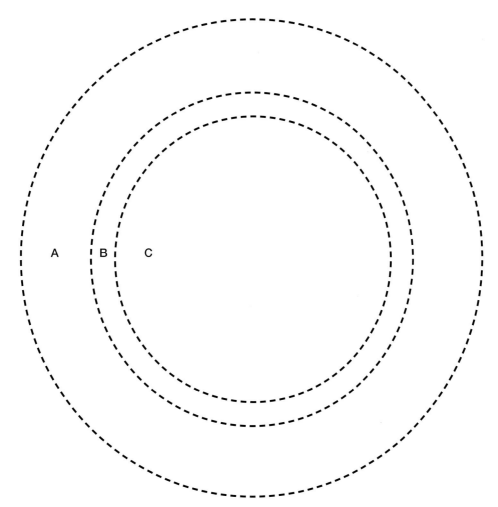

1. Photocopy or trace this page 3 times.
2. Cut along outer rim of dotted lines on template **A.**
3. Cut along outer rim of dotted lines on template **B.**
4. Cut along outer rim of dotted lines on template **C.**
5. Ice cake with Vanilla buttercream icing, then position circles on cake according to positioning guide.
6. Follow instructions on cake card in back pocket.

Positioning Guide

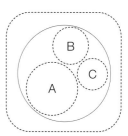

FATHER'S DAY FUN

Positioning Guide

1. Photocopy or trace this page twice, so that there are two templates for the letter D.
2. Cut out letters along dotted lines. Fold templates along centerlines to make cutting out center of letters easier.
3. Ice cake with Chocolate buttercream icing, then position templates D-A-D on cake according to positioning guide.
4. Follow instructions on cake card in back pocket.

4TH OF JULY PINWHEEL

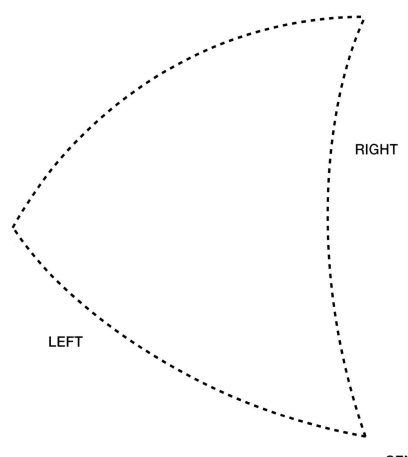

RIGHT

LEFT

CENTER

Positioning Guide

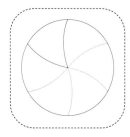

1. Photocopy or trace this page.
2. Cut along dotted lines.
3. Ice cake with Vanilla buttercream icing, then position template on cake according to positioning guide. You will use this template 6 times to create a clockwise pinwheel on the top of the cake.
4. Follow instructions on cake card in back pocket.

HALLOWEEN CANDY-CAKE

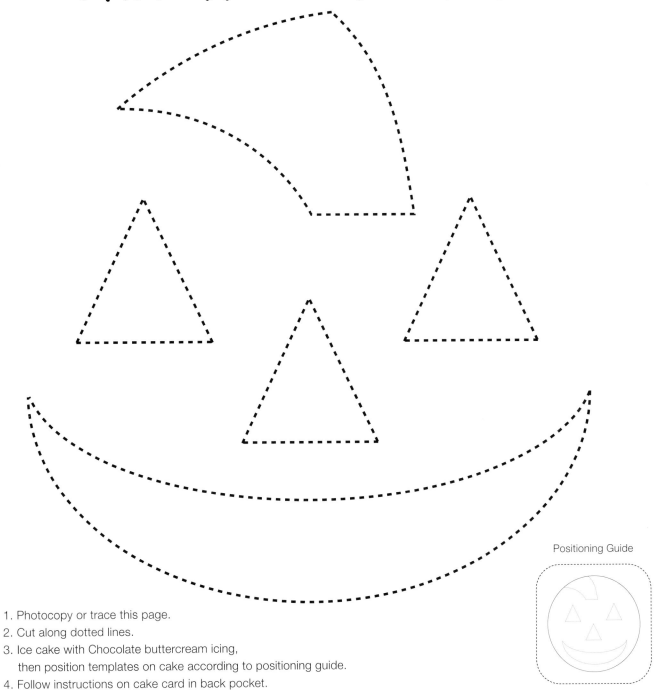

Positioning Guide

1. Photocopy or trace this page.
2. Cut along dotted lines.
3. Ice cake with Chocolate buttercream icing,
   then position templates on cake according to positioning guide.
4. Follow instructions on cake card in back pocket.

RAINY DAY CAKE

1. Photocopy or trace this page.
2. Cut along dotted lines.
3. Ice cake with Vanilla buttercream icing,
   then position template on cake according to positioning guide.
4. Follow instructions on cake card in back pocket.

Positioning Guide

VALENTINE'S DAY HEARTS

A   B   C

1. Photocopy or trace this page.
2. Fold template along center line for easy cutting.
3. Cut along dotted lines. Discard template **B**.
4. Ice cake with Cotton Candy Pink buttercream icing,
   then position templates **A** and **C** on cake according to positioning guide.
5. Follow instructions on cake card in back pocket.

Positioning Guide

A

C